PU

INDIRA

H.Y. Sharada Prasad was media advisor to both Indira Gandhi and Rajiv Gandhi, serving in the Prime Minister's Office from 1966–1978, and then again from 1980–1988.

Educated at Mysore University and jailed during the Quit India Movement, he began his professional life as a journalist. His other works include *Rashtrapati Bhavan:The Story of the President's House* and *Exploring Karnataka*; besides a large number of translations and anthologies. He also edited the *Selected Works of Jawaharlal Nehru*. H.Y. Sharada Prasad was honoured with the Padma Bhushan in 2000 and the Indira Gandhi Award for National Integration in 2001. He passed away in 2008.

INDIRA GANDHI

by H.Y. SHARADA PRASAD

With a foreword by RAJIV GANDHI

PUFFIN BOOKS

PUFFIN BOOKS

First published by Ladybird Books Ltd 1986

Penguin Books India Pvt. Ltd, 11 Community Centre, Panchsheel Park, New Delhi 110 017, India

Penguin Group (USA) Inc., 375 Hudson Street, New York, New York 10014, USA

Penguin Group (Canada), 90 Eglinton Avenue East, Suite 700, Toronto, Ontario, M4P 2Y3, Canada (a division of Pearson Penguin Canada Inc.)

Penguin Books Ltd, 80 Strand, London WC2R 0RL, England

Penguin Ireland, 25 St Stephen's Green, Dublin 2, Ireland (a division of Penguin Books Ltd)

Penguin Group (Australia), 707 Collins Street, Melbourne, Victoria 3008, Australia (a division of Pearson Australia Group Pty Ltd)

Penguin Group (NZ), 67 Apollo Drive, Rosedale, Auckland 0632, New Zealand (a division of Pearson New Zealand Ltd)

Penguin Group (South Africa) (Pty) Ltd, 24 Sturdee Avenue, Rosebank, Johannesburg 2196, South Africa

Penguin Books Ltd, Registered Offices: 80 Strand, London WC2R 0RL, England

First published by Ladybird Books Ltd 1986
First published in Puffin by Penguin Books India 2013
Copyright @ Indira Gandhi Memorial Trust 2013

10 9 8 7 6 5 4 3 2 1

ISBN 9780143332886

Typeset in Sabon MT by Eleven Arts, Delhi
Printed at Manipal Technologies Ltd, Manipal

ALWAYS LEARNING   **PEARSON**

Prime Minister
FOREWORD

Everyone spends the early years with a very special person—one's mother. My own mother was unusual. She later became Prime Minister of India and famous all over the world, as this book will tell you. Even when I and my younger brother were small, she did a great amount of work for the country. But she spent a good deal of time with us, and took care to make it exciting. She never put on airs of being important or busy. She was full of games and puzzles and stories and bits of poetry. She knew a great deal about history, about books, about art and about trees and birds. She made us feel we were her equal. She refrained from lecturing or giving advice and encouraged us to discuss matters with her. She let us take our own decisions. Later, when I grew up, I regarded her as a friend rather than as someone twenty-six years older.

One of her favourite statements was that a person who was interested became interesting.

She remained a great learner—always trying to understand new ideas and re-examine the old.

The world fascinated her. She believed in being mentally and physically alert all the time. That is how she was able to do the work of a dozen people.

I hope this book will help you to understand how Indira Gandhi was spurred from her childhood by the ideal of freedom and a determination to serve the people of India and the whole world.

(RAJIV GANDHI)

New Delhi
September 27, 1985

Indira Gandhi was born on 19 November 1917 in Allahabad, one of India's ancient cities, where the Yamuna River flows into the Ganges. She was born in the house of her grandfather, Motilal Nehru.

In Motilal's day, India was part of the British Empire, and Motilal himself lived like a British gentleman, in a large house set in lush, sprawling grounds. He was fond of western clothes and western food. He engaged British governesses for his two daughters and a British tutor for his only son, Jawaharlal.

Anand Bhawan, the Nehru family home.

Motilal, a strong-willed, high-spirited, generous man known for his laughter and anger, was very fond of his son, and very proud of him. When Jawaharlal was fifteen, Motilal sent him to Harrow, a public school in England. From there he went to Cambridge University.

Motilal Nehru.

The boy Jawaharlal on a bicycle.

After Cambridge, Jawaharlal studied law, and then returned to India. However, his heart was not in a legal career. Instead, he was deeply interested in politics—and in how to free India from British rule.

In 1916 Jawaharlal married Kamala Kaul. The wedding took

Jawaharlal's mother, Swarup Rani.

Jawaharlal Nehru with his parents.

Kamala Nehru.

place in Delhi, the capital of India. Motilal and the large party of guests booked a whole train to travel to Delhi. The festivities went on for several days.

Kamala was a shy bride. She was not very familiar with English or western customs or manners. It took

Jawaharlal and Kamala at their wedding.

time for her to adjust to the ways of Anand
Bhawan, or Abode of Joy, as Motilal called
his house.

When their daughter was born the
following year, Jawaharlal and Kamala called
her Indira. They gave her a second name as
well—Priyadarshini, or 'dear to behold'.

Within two years of Indira's birth the
entire way of life changed at Anand Bhawan.
Mahatma Gandhi had become the leader

*Indira as a baby
with her parents.*

The Nehru family. Indira at the centre on her grandmother's lap.

of India's nationalist movement, and the Nehrus—especially Indira's father and grandfather—became his dedicated followers.

After the First World War, Gandhi had hoped that India would be given a greater degree of self-government. He was disappointed with what the British government offered, and began to organize national protests. He taught that the British should be opposed non-violently—not with weapons, but by organizing people all over the country to disobey civil laws, to refuse to pay taxes and to boycott British goods. Such action was called *satyagraha*.

India in those days imported large quantities of cloth from Britain. Gandhi urged his followers to learn to spin, and to wear cloth made by hand as a sign that the people of India would be self-reliant and not dependent on the goods of other countries. Gandhi and the Indian National Congress (India's leading political party) organized bonfires of British cloth. The Nehrus, known for the stylish clothes they wore, sent their woollens and chiffons to the flames, and everyone at Anand Bhawan began to wear homespun.

When she was about four, Indira was given a beautiful doll made in England. Though she loved it dearly, she finally decided she must give it up. Years later she described her feelings this way:

Indira with her dolls.

'For days on end the struggle went on between my love for my doll and what I thought to be my

*duty towards my country . . . At last I made
my decision and, quivering with tension, I
took the doll up on the roof-terrace and set
fire to it. Then the tears came as if they would
never stop and for some days I was ill. To this
day I hate striking a match.'*

Several times during the struggle for
freedom Indira's father was arrested and put
in prison. In fact, over the next twenty-five

years, Jawaharlal
spent nearly ten
years in jail.

Indira's mother
had a baby boy,
but he did not live
long. Kamala, who
had always been
somewhat frail,
developed a lung
disease and in 1926
went to Switzerland
for treatment.
Indira, who was
eight years old at
the time, went with
her. They stayed

Indira in khadi.

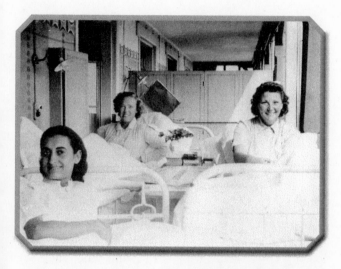

Indira with the sanatorium staff in Switzerland.

in Geneva for some months, where Indira
attended the International School. She then
attended a school in the nearby town of Bex.

Indira's father was a great reader and
Anand Bhawan was always full of books. Indira
loved reading from the time she was very young.
She read stories and poems, but what she loved
most was reading about men and women who
had fought for their countries—Joan of Arc
of France, Garibaldi of Italy, Simón Bolívar of
South America. She identified herself with Joan

Indira in Geneva.

of Arc because she too was a girl who had stood against British domination.

Jawaharlal often gave Indira challenging books to read. He was also keen that she should be physically fit. Indira had to run and do exercises regularly. She learnt to swim. When the family went to the hills to escape the heat of Allahabad's summer, Indira was so nimble at climbing rocks that her grandfather called her 'mountain goat'. Mountain trekking remained a passion with Indira throughout her life. She was also fond of skiing.

At home in Allahabad, Indira had her hands full. Mahatma Gandhi was often there, as were other leaders of the Congress. Indira was kept busy running errands for them and shielding

Indira at Bhowali.

them from the public. When there were riots or other disturbances, the injured were brought to Anand Bhawan where Kamala, Indira and others cleaned and bandaged their wounds.

Indira was loved but not spoilt. Because she was gawky and long-nosed, some of her relations called her an ugly duckling. Often left on her own, she learnt to take her own decisions. She was intense and had a searching,

questioning mind. But above all she wanted
to be worthy of her parents, and to help and
protect them. She was proud that their pictures,
along with pictures of Mahatma Gandhi, were
found in hundreds of thousands of homes.

When Indira was twelve years old, her
father became President of the Indian National
Congress. At its 1929 session, the Congress
had declared that it wanted nothing less than
complete independence. Though she was still
very young, Indira was one of those who took
the pledge of independence which declared:

*The British government in India has not only
deprived the Indian people of their freedom
but has based itself on the exploitation of the
masses, and has ruined India economically,
politically, culturally and spiritually. We believe,
therefore, that India must sever the British
connection.*

When told that she had to be eighteen
to become a member of the Congress Party,
Indira decided to form her own organization.
She gathered together a large number of
boys and girls and launched the Vanar Sena
or Monkey Brigade. Its members helped the

freedom movement by sewing Congress Party flags, cooking food for people who took part in demonstrations, giving first aid to workers injured in police conflicts and so on.

Like all fathers, Jawaharlal was fond of giving advice. The advice he gave Indira on her thirteenth birthday was:

'It is no easy matter to decide what is right and what is not. One little test I shall ask you to apply whenever you are in doubt. Never do anything in secret or anything that you would wish to hide. For the desire to hide anything means that you are afraid, and fear is a bad thing and unworthy of you. Be brave, and all the rest follows.'

Just six weeks later, on the last day of 1930, a mysterious caller telephoned to say that Indira's mother would soon be arrested. Jawaharlal had been in jail for some months, and his wife had been playing an active part in the fight for freedom. On New Year's Eve she and Indira ate dinner together and then read aloud poetry by Tennyson. Early the next morning the police came to take Kamala Nehru away.

Jawaharlal Nehru (c. 1920).

Only a few weeks after that Motilal, the old warrior, passed away. Jawaharlal and Kamala had just come out of jail.

A year later Indira's father was back in prison. Over the next eighteen months he wrote letters to Indira relating the stories of the various peoples of the world. He described how some nations had oppressed others and how people struggled for freedom and equality. The letters—196 in all—were later published under the title *Glimpses of World History*. What Jawaharlal wrote stayed with Indira all her life.

After her grandfather's death, Indira was sent to a school in Poona, a thousand miles away from Allahabad. It was an unusual school. Its name, the Pupils' Own School, gave some clue as to how it was run. The children were expected to think for themselves and be independent. They visited areas where poor people lived, and helped the people they visited. They did not work all the time, however. Indira learnt to dance and took part in plays at the Pupils' Own School, too.

After leaving school, Indira went to the Visva-Bharati University, in the east of India. The university had been founded by

Rabindranath Tagore, painter, musician, poet and playwright, who had won the Nobel Prize for Literature. Tagore believed that education should produce a 'universal' human being, one who was well developed culturally and artistically as well as intellectually. Here Indira came to know people of outstanding talent.

But Indira did not stay long at Visva-Bharati. Her mother's health was failing.

Kamala Nehru during her illness.

Indira with Tagore at Shantiniketan.

Kamala was advised to go to Europe again for treatment, and Indira travelled with her.

It proved to be Kamala's last illness. She died in February 1936. It was some comfort to the family that Jawaharlal had been able to fly to Europe to be with her at the end. She was thirty-six and Indira was eighteen. It took Indira a long time to recover from the loss.

In 1938, Indira entered Somerville College, Oxford. Those who studied with her remember her as a quiet but strong-willed person. Once someone asked her why she was studying in

Indira in Europe.

Britain when India was fighting the British. She
answered, 'So as to know the adversary better.'
She worked for the India League, which put
forward India's case for freedom in Britain.

Indian freedom was not the only cause
that kept Indira busy. She collected funds for
China, which had been attacked by Japan, and
attended meetings to protest against the Nazis.

One of the reasons Indira decided to study
in England was that Feroze Gandhi was there.
Feroze, five years older than Indira, was also
from Allahabad. Politics excited him and he
had helped Kamala Nehru in her work. He had
proposed to Indira when she was only sixteen
but she had turned him down. Feroze did not
give up. He and Indira met again in Europe,
and his persistence paid off.

But Indira fell seriously ill. She was advised
to go to Switzerland for rest. Within a few days
of her arrival there, the Second World War
broke out. Britain was cut off. It was many
months before Indira could return to England,
and then only after a long wait in Portugal. She
filled her time by teaching English to refugees.

She and Feroze left England and sailed for
India in 1941. On the way, their ship docked in
South Africa, where Indira was angered by the

laws imposing bans against black people. She made a fiery speech against racialism.

Indira and Feroze were married on 26 March 1942 at Anand Bhawan. They observed the old Hindu wedding ritual of going round the sacred fire seven times, although Feroze was not a Hindu. He was a Parsi, a follower of the ancient religion of Zoroastrianism. And though his surname was Gandhi, he was no relation to Mahatma Gandhi.

Among the wedding gifts were two that Indira prized in particular—a piece of cloth woven by Mahatma Gandhi and a sari made from yarn that had been spun by her father.

There was great political tension in India at the time. The war was not going too well for Britain and the Allies. Japan had overrun country after country and was moving close to India. The Indian National Congress demanded the right to defend itself. The British turned down the demand. Self-government only after victory, they said. Freedom now, insisted Mahatma Gandhi. He planned a new *satyagraha* to make the British quit India. But the British arrested Mahatma Gandhi, Jawaharlal Nehru and all the top leaders of Congress as well as thousands of other people all over the country.

Indira Gandhi at a political meeting.

Feroze and Indira, who were in Bombay, went back to Allahabad to organize resistance. It was announced that Indira would address a rally there. Policemen and soldiers were all around as the crowd gathered. Feroze watched from a nearby building. When Indira began her speech he saw her surrounded by police, with a bayonet almost touching her. He rushed out at the policemen. Both Feroze and Indira were taken to the Allahabad jail. There they spent the next few months, but apart from each other—she in the women's section of the prison and he in the men's wing.

Indira was not allowed to receive letters or have visitors. She, therefore, had no link with her father. But she was determined not to be defeated. Eight months later she came out of jail. *'It was like coming suddenly out of a dark passage. I was dazzled with the rush of life, the many hues and textures, the scale of sounds and the range of ideas,'* she said.

Six months later Feroze was released, and they set up house together once again. On 20 August 1944 their first son, Rajiv, was born. Jawaharlal, who was still in jail, wrote very solicitous letters, giving Indira advice and suggesting names for his grandson. Indira said the birth of Rajiv was the happiest moment in her life. Of motherhood she said: *'To bring a new being into this world, to see its tiny perfection, and to dream of its future greatness is the most moving of all experiences.'*

Jawaharlal Nehru and the leaders of the

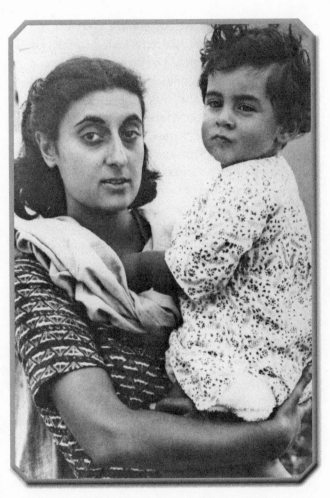

Indira Gandhi with Rajiv.

Congress were freed in the middle of 1945.
Mahatma Gandhi had been released earlier. The
war was about to end. The British knew they
could not hold India much longer. They opened
negotiations with the leaders of the Congress.
At the same time the Muslim League, another
of India's political parties, demanded that a
separate state of Pakistan should be created,
made up of those areas of India where Muslims
were in the majority. Until the issue was resolved
an interim government of Indian leaders was
formed, with Jawaharlal Nehru at its head.

Jawaharlal wanted Indira to look after his
household. Indira took to dividing her time
between her father in Delhi and her husband in

Pandit Nehru at the time of transfer of power.

Lucknow. Her second son, Sanjay, was born in
December 1946.

   The attempts to prevent the splitting of
India failed. India and Pakistan came into being
as separate dominions—India at midnight
of 14 August 1947 and Pakistan a few hours
earlier. Lord Mountbatten, the last Viceroy of
India, read the British monarch's proclamation
of India's freedom. And, in a speech that
became famous, Jawaharlal Nehru declared:
*'Long years ago we made a tryst with destiny,
and now the time comes when we shall redeem*

Sanjay Gandhi with Feroze Gandhi.

Indira Gandhi with Rajiv and Sanjay.

our pledge . . . At the stroke of the midnight hour, when the world sleeps, India will awake to life and freedom.' Jawaharlal Nehru became the first Prime Minister of free India.

Because the country was partitioned, millions of people moved from Pakistan to

Indira Gandhi with Rajiv and Sanjay in Paris.

The Red Fort, Delhi on Independence Day, 1947.

India and from India to Pakistan. They were
filled with fear and hate, and hundreds of
thousands were killed. At Mahatma Gandhi's
request, Indira went to work in the riot-torn
areas of Delhi, helping people in need and
attempting to calm the troubled atmosphere.
She worked hard and tirelessly, and Mahatma
Gandhi praised her dedication. But that man of
peace was himself killed by a fanatic just a few
months later.

Indira was finally persuaded to stay in Delhi
and be her father's hostess. For years she had
acted as his secretary, typed letters for him and
travelled with him. She had read the proofs of the
book he wrote in his final term of imprisonment,

*Indira Gandhi on the train with the ashes of
Mahatma Gandhi.*

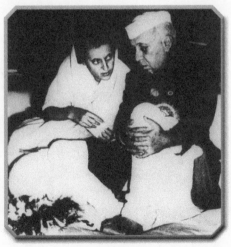

*Indira Gandhi with Pandit Nehru at the AICC
session, 1961.*

Pandit Nehru with Rajiv and Sanjay.

Indira Gandhi at Rajiv's birthday party.

Pandit Nehru, Indira Gandhi, Rajiv and Sanjay.

Indira Gandhi and Pandit Nehru at dining table.

Indira Gandhi with Pandit Nehru, Dehradun on 26 May 1964, the day before his death.

Rajiv and Sanjay with Pandit Nehru's ashes.

The Discovery of India. Now there were international statesmen to meet and foreign countries to visit. She also had her little sons to take care of. She set aside as much time as she could to be with them. A mother's company, she said, was like water and air to a child.

But politics did not leave her alone. Indira was inducted into the main committees of the Congress Party, and in 1959 she was elected its President.

In September 1960 Feroze died of a heart attack. Within four years Jawaharlal Nehru was also dead. He had been Prime Minister of India for seventeen years. Indira Gandhi hoped that she could now retire to the high mountains. But the new Prime Minister, Lal Bahadur Shastri, would not hear of it. He insisted that she join his cabinet. She was given charge of the Ministry of Information and Broadcasting.

Shastri's stay in office was short. Early in January 1966 he died unexpectedly. Once again the country had to find a new Prime Minister. The leaders of the Congress thought that Indira would be the best choice. The other contender for the post was Morarji Desai. Indira easily won the election, and she was sworn in as

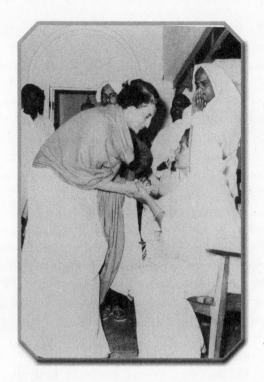

Indira Gandhi with Lalita Shastri.

Prime Minister on 24 January 1966. She was to
remain in that office for eleven years.

In the 1967 general election, Indira's party,
the Congress, was returned to power but
with a reduced majority. Some of the policies

Indira Gandhi inspecting the floods in Assam.

adopted by Indira Gandhi were opposed by
her colleagues, and there was a split within the
party. Indira Gandhi's wing won a huge victory
in the 1971 elections.

But one of the candidates who had opposed
her went to court saying that she had won the
election unfairly. The case went on for four
years. In June 1975 her election was set aside
but the court ruled that she might continue to
be Prime Minister. Still, several political parties
demanded her resignation. Some of them asked
the police and the army to revolt, as in their
view Indira Gandhi had lost the moral right

Indira Gandhi addressing a public meeting.

to be Prime Minister. She placed the country
under a state of emergency, arresting a large
number of opposition leaders and workers, and
introduced censorship of the press.

Twenty-one months later, in March 1977,
Indira Gandhi called for an election. Her
faith was in the people's right to decide.
But much that had happened during the
emergency was not to the liking of the
people. Her party was soundly defeated.
The opposition leaders who had been
jailed by her won by large margins. Various
opposition parties merged to form a single

party, the Janata Party.
The new government
appointed a commission
to inquire into Indira
Gandhi's actions. Her
younger son, Sanjay, who
had become prominent
in national politics
during the emergency,
was arrested.

*Indira Gandhi after
an election victory.*

It was not long before
the tide of people's
sympathy began flowing
back towards Indira
Gandhi. She won a by-
election to the Lok Sabha,
one of the houses of
Parliament. However, the
House expelled her and
she had to spend some
days in jail.

The groups which
had formed the Janata
Party broke up. The
new government was
compelled to call a general
election halfway through

*Indira Gandhi at
the time of Sanjay's
death.*

Family portraits.

its five-year term. In the January 1980 polls for the Lok Sabha, Indira Gandhi was swept back to power.

Within six months, tragedy struck her. Sanjay was killed while flying an aircraft. Indira bore the blow with great calm.

Despite her popularity, Indira Gandhi, like all political leaders, had her share of enemies. On the morning of 31 October 1984, as Indira came out onto the lawns of her house for a television interview, her enemies shot her dead. She was nineteen days short of her sixty-seventh birthday.

Indira Gandhi died as she would have wanted to, active until the last minute. For years she had worked sixteen hours a day, rarely taking holidays. Her energy, even when she was in her sixties, amazed people. She was fond of saying that there was a vast store of power within everyone but people failed to recognize and develop it.

Her grandchildren found her fun to be with. She had a wide range of interests: painting, folk music, dance, poetry, flowers and birds, the conservation of nature. She believed that life could not be broken up into compartments, and that in order to achieve

Indira Gandhi with the Bharat Ratna.

Indira Gandhi with her pets.

Indira Gandhi at a press conference.

Indira Gandhi with a tiger.

Pandit Nehru and Indira Gandhi with President Kennedy.

Indira Gandhi and Pandit Nehru with Subhash Chandra Bose.

Pandit Nehru with Indira Gandhi in London.

Indira Gandhi, with Sheikh Muzibur Rehman.

Indira Gandhi with chiefs of the armed forces.

Indira Gandhi with her grandchildren.

Indira Gandhi with her grandchildren.

inner poise, one must know the unity of all living things.

Her guiding principle was to do her duty, unmindful of whether the fruit was bitter or sweet. Only the evening before her death she had spoken to a large gathering, a thousand miles away from Delhi, and said:

'I am here today, but I may not be here tomorrow. Nobody knows how many attempts

Indira Gandhi.

have been made to shoot me. I do not care
whether I live or die. I have enjoyed a long life
and I am proud that I spent the whole of it in
the service of my people. I shall continue to
serve until my last breath. And when I die, I can
say that every drop of my blood will invigorate
India and strengthen it.'

Indira Gandhi was fond of a poem by
Rabindranath Tagore. Not happy with English
translations by others, she wrote her own. And
here it is:

> *If no one listens to your call,*
> *Walk alone.*
> *If in fear they cower, mutely facing the wall,*
> *O hapless one,*
> *Open your mind and speak out alone.*
> *If, as you cross the wilderness, they turn away*
> *and desert you,*
> *O hapless one,*
> *Tread firmly on the thorns among the blood-*
> *lined track, and travel alone.*
> *If, in the storm-troubled night, they dare not*
> *hold aloft the light,*
> *O hapless one,*
> *Ignite your own heart with the lightning and*
> *pain, and yourself become the guiding light.*